Disney

M⊚ANA

Hairstyles & Looks

EDDA USA

MOANA HAIRSTYLES & LOOKS
© 2016 Disney Enterprises, Inc.

Author: Cynthia Littlefield
Photographer: Gassi Olafsson
Stylist: Magnea Einarsdottir
Hairdresser: Theodora Mjoll Skuladottir
Layout and design: Baddydesign, www.baddydesign.com
Cover design: Baddydesign, www.baddydesign.com

Printed in Canada

ISBN: 978-1-94078-774-9

www.eddausa.com

Distributed by Macmillan

List of Contents

Get Curls like Moana

Do you want to get curly hair like Moana's? Try these fun and easy no-heat techniques for gorgeous curly tresses!

To increase the longevity of the looks when you're done, you can flip your hair upside down and spray it lightly with hairspray.

Technique 1: Braids in wet hair

Wash your hair and, after lightly towel-drying it, comb it and put it in braids. The size of the braids would depend on the size you want for your curls; if you want big curls, only do one or two braids, if you prefer smaller curls, do several smaller braids all over.

Leave the hair in the braids as it dries, preferably overnight. When you remove the braids from the dry hair, only use your fingers to seperate it. You should now have gorgeous curly locks!

Technique 2: Paper towels in wet hair

If you want to try a different technique, you could also wrap your freshly washed, towel-dried hair in paper towels or clean rags that you've torn from a soft cloth, such as an old sheet. The strips should be 1–5 inches wide and 8–18 inches long.

Divide your hair into sections, the size of which depends on the size you want for your curls. Fold the rag or paper towel over a section of the hair and roll it towards your scalp. Tie the loose ends of the rag once you've reached the scalp. Repeat all around the head.

When your hair is completely dry, gently take out the rags and reveal your beautiful new curls!

Fabulous Braids

Crosscurrent Plait

1. Section off a large square of hair at the top of the head, then tie the rest of the hair out of the way for now (photo A).

2. Unbind the top square, and part off a band of hair at the hairline. Divide the band into three parts (photo B) and weave them together as you would to start a classic braid.

3. Continue braiding toward the back of the head, picking up sections from both sides as you would to create a French braid (photos C & D).

4. When you reach the back and all the hair from the top of the head has been incorporated, bind the braid with a hair elastic, leaving a long tail (photo E).

5. Gently loosen the sections of the braid to make it fuller.

6. Lift a thin strand of hair from the braid tail and wrap it around the elastic, then bind the end with another elastic and spread the wrapped portion to cover both bands (photo F).

A  B  C 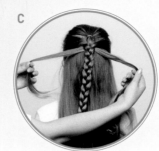 D

Threaded Back Braid

1. Gather the hair at the top of the head and bind it at the upper back with an elastic. Braid the hair below the elastic and bind the tail with another elastic (photo A).

2. Lift a small section of hair from the right side (near the face) and pull it back toward the braid. Thread the end of the section through the top right loop of the braid (photo B).

3. Repeat step 2 with a section of hair from the left side, tucking the end into the top left loop of the braid (photo C). Continue in this manner, lifting small sections (alternating from one side to the other) and threading them through the subsequent loops of the braid until you reach the braid tail (photo D). Then bind all the ends together with another elastic.

A   B   C

Twined Tresses

1. Gather matching thin hanks of hair from the hairline at the temples. Pull them toward the back of the head, twisting the one from the left side clockwise and the one from the right counterclockwise. Bind them together behind the head with a small hair elastic (photo A).

2. Gather a second pair of hanks right below the first set, twisting them in the same manner. Bind them together directly below the first elastic (photo B).

3. Twist and bind a third set below the first two.

4. Continue in this manner to create three more rows, or until you reach the nape of the neck (photo C).

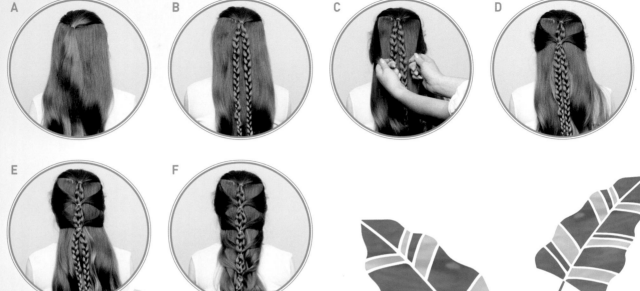

Pacific Lace

1. Gather two small locks of hair from the hairline at the center of the forehead, and bind them together at the top of the head with a small elastic (photo A).

2. Divide the ponytail into two and braid each of the two sections (photo B).

3. Gather a second set of locks from the hairline, at the sides of the face, and bind them to the two small braids, a few inches below the first elastic (photos C and D).

4. Repeat with a third set of locks (photo E) and continue until a few inches above the end of the hair (photo F).

A   B   C   D

E   F   G   H

I

Tideline Twist

1. Divide the hair into two equal sections at the nape (photo A).

2. Lift a long lock from the section on the right (photo B), and weave it under the section on the left (photo C).

3. Next, wrap the same lock over the left section and under the right section (photo D).

4. Repeat steps 2 & 3 until you only have a small tail of the lock left (photos E & F). Bind the tail with a small hair elastic tucked up tight against the last full twist.

5. Lift another long lock from the right section and continue the over-and-under weave (photos G & H), beginning it snugly against the first portion and binding the end as you did before.

*** You can leave the weave straight (as is), or for a variation, gently twist it clockwise once or twice. This variation would be named Waterspout.

Amazing Knots & Updos

Wayfinder's Knot

1. Gather a section of hair from the left side of the head and shape it into a loop at the back of the head — be sure that the tail is UNDER the loop — and use a clip to hold it in place (photo A).

2. Gather a section from the right side of the head and cross it over the loop and under the tail. Re-clip the hair to hold it in place (photo B).

3. Lift the tail of the right section and thread it up through the upper portion of the loop (photo C). Then thread it over the cross section and back down through the lower portion of the loop (photo D).

4. Gently pull the ends to shape and tighten the knot a bit (photo E).

5. Combine the tail on the right with a small section of loose hair from the right side of the head, and bind them together with a hair elastic (photos F & G). Repeat with the tail on the left side (photos H & I).

Two Part Heart

1. Gather a section of hair from the hairline above the ear on both sides, and bind the two sections together with a hair elastic at the upper back of the head (photo A).

2. Working on one side of the head, lift a second section of hair from the hairline just below the first section (photo B).

3. Pull the new section toward the back of the head, then loop it up and over the first section just above the hair elastic (photo C).

4. Lift a matching section from the other side of the head and repeat steps 2 & 3 to create another loop opposite the first one (photo D).

5. Bind the tails from both loops to the center tail with another hair elastic, creating a heart shape against the back of the head (photos E & F).

A

B

C

D

E

F

Knot Weave

1. Divide the hair at the top of the head into two sections and tie them into a half knot at the upper back of the head (photo A). Use clips to hold the ends in place for now (photo B) and bobby-pin the knot itself to secure it, if needed.

2. Gather two more sections of hair below the first pair and add them to the ends of the half knot (photo C). Tie another half knot (photo D), again using bobby pins to secure it.

3. Continue in this manner, adding new sections of hair from the sides and tying two more half knots (photo E).

4. Using the ends from the last (fourth) half knot, tie a final half knot around the remaining middle section of hair. Bind the ends with a hair elastic right below the last half knot, and decorate the end with a silk flower if you like (photo F).

Heart of Te Fiti Bun

1. Section off a large square of hair at the top of the head. Then gather all the rest of the hair in a high ponytail at the back of the crown (photo A).

2. Lift a hank of hair from the square and a matching hank from the ponytail (photo B). Cross the left hank over the right one (photo C).

3. Gather another hank from the ponytail. Cross it over the hank from the square and add it to the first hank from the ponytail (photo D).

4. Cross another hank from the square over the last one, and add it to the hank on the right (photo E).

5. Repeat steps 3 and 4, adding hair from one side to the other, until you've incorporated all the hair from the square into the weave (photo F).

6. At this point you should have two sections of hair, the woven section to the left and roughly half of the ponytail to the right. Continue weaving the hair, herringbone-style, adding hair from one side to the other and vice versa until the remaining ponytail is incorporated, then bind the end with a hair elastic (photo G).

7. Lift the braid tail upward and, counterclockwise, tuck it well into the opening just above the ponytail elastic (photos H & I). Bobby-pin the bun to hold it in place (photo J).

Easy and Fun Hair Accessories

Leafy Bun Wrap

Inspired by the lush leafy vegetation on Motunui, this flexible wrap adds a colorful and whimsical twist to a hair bun or ponytail.

Materials:

- Five 9- by 12-inch pieces of prewashed solid or printed cotton fabric in shades of green, red, and yellow for the leaves
- Five 6- by 9-inch pieces of double-sided fusible webbing
- Steam iron and pressing cloth
- Leafy Bun Wrap Template
- Straight pins for pinning the template
- Fabric or craft scissors
- 3- by 19-inch strip of prewashed solid or printed green cotton fabric for the bun wrap base
- 18-inch strip of double-sided ½-inch fusible tape
- 18-inch cloth-covered floral wire stem
- Crafting pliers
- Fabric or tacky glue

Instructions:

1. To make the leaves for the bun wrap, cut each of the five fabric rectangles into two 6- by 9-inch pieces. Fuse each pair together (right sides facing out), using a piece of the double-sided webbing following the manufacturer's directions. Be sure to use the pressing cloth to keep any of the webbing from melting onto the iron.

2. Using the Leafy Bun Wrap Template, found in the back of this book, make a photocopy of it and carefully cut out the shape of the leaf. This will be your master template. Trace the leaf onto the fused fabric and cut around it. You will need about 15 leaves in all. Tip: As an alternative, you can substitute all or a few of the leaves with faux leaves purchased from the floral section of your local craft store.

3. Once you've cut out all the leaves you need, fold and press each one down the middle to create a center crease. Set the leaves aside for now.

4. To create the base of the bun wrap, fold both long edges of the 3- by 19-inch fabric strip over ½ inch and press them. Then fold the short ends over ½ inch and press them. Now fold the fabric in half to create a long 1-inch band and press well to create a good crease.

5. Unfold the band and adhere an 18-inch strip of fusible tape to each of the long edges, again using the pressing cloth and following the manufacturer's directions. Once the underside of each tape is adhered to the fabric, remove the protective paper from its surface to expose the sticky top.

6. Arrange the leaves along the tape on the upper edge of the band, starting at one side and going all the way to the other. Overlap the leaves slightly and make sure the bottoms line up along the center crease to keep them from flopping over when the wrap is complete.

Flower Bloom Hair Clip

Natural fibers from the Pacific island trees, like the mulberry tree, have long been used to create beautiful textiles and paper by the people of Motunui. This bold clip-on floral hair ornament combines the rich textures of paper, twine, and wood.

Materials:

- Set of 3 multi-sized flower-shaped cookie or fondant cutters (about 2, 2½, and 3 inches)
- Pencil
- Craft paper (assorted shades and patterns of browns and off-white)
- Glue sealer and small paintbrush or foam brush to apply it
- Craft scissors
- Glue sealer
- Tacky glue
- Toothpick
- Decorative wooden button (or one made from another natural material)
- Pushpin
- Natural-colored twine (thin enough to thread 2 or 3 strands through the buttonholes)
- Pinch-style hair clip small enough to attach to the back of the flower without showing

Instructions:

1. Trace each of the three cookie cutters onto different pieces of craft paper. Cut out the tracings and brush a coat of glue sealer on each one, front and back.

2. Once the sealer is completely dry, center the cutouts atop one another. Use the tip of the toothpick to apply a few drops of glue between the layers to hold the pieces in place.

3. Use the pushpin to poke two holes through the center of the assembled blossom, spacing them the same distance apart as the buttonholes. Wiggle the pin to broaden the holes a bit.

4. Thread the ends of two or three 5-inch lengths of twine up through the holes in the blossom and then through the buttonholes. Tie all the ends together to hold the button snugly against the flower center. Trim the trailing twine to vary them slightly in length and then tie an overhead knot near the end of each.

5. Cut out a paper circle about the width of the smallest flower layer and spread glue on the back. Open the clip and hold the top half against the back of the blossom, then stick the circle to the blossom, sandwiching the clip top firmly between them. Hold the pieces together briefly until the glue begins to set and then let it dry completely before wearing the clip.

Pearl-Topped Bobby Pins

Pearls are abundant in the waters surrounding Motunui. These pearly pins look elegant slipped into random locks of a braid or tucked into a bun. You can make them with any color faux pearl beads you like, but cream-colored ones are especially nice with the silver wire.

Materials:
- 5/16-inch faux pearl beads
- 26-gauge silver-plaited copper jewelry wire
- Bobby pins
- Jewelry pliers/wire cutters

Instructions:

1. For each bobby pin, thread a pearl bead onto the center of an 8-inch length of jewelry wire.

2. Hold the bead on the top of a bobby pin and thread the wire ends through the bobby pin top from opposite directions. Pull the ends upward and thread them back through the pearl, one from left to right, and the other vice versa.

3. Individually wrap each of the wire ends around the nearest bobby pin prong four or five times. Then, bring the two wires together and wrap them snuggly around the bobby pin top right below the pearl a few times.

4. Cut off any extra from the wire ends, and use the pliers to lightly pinch the wound wire just enough to hold it in place.

Button Hair Comb

Moana was just a young girl when she first discovered the beautiful shells that dot the Pacific Ocean floor surrounding Motunui. Topped with shiny shell or pearl buttons, this hand-decorated hair comb is a tribute to the bountiful sea.

Materials:

- 26-gauge silver-plaited copper jewelry wire
- Jewelry pliers/wire cutters
- 3 to 5 flower-shape shell or pearl buttons (ranging from 3/8 to 1 inch wide)
- Hair comb
- Small craft scissors
- 1 coconut husk or wooden round button (about 5/8 inch wide) to use as a center for each of the larger (1-inch) buttons
- Tacky glue

Instructions:

1. Thread the ends of an 8-inch length of the jewelry wire down through the center of one of the buttons. Attach the button to the comb by wrapping the wire ends around the top between the teeth a couple of times. Then wind one end clockwise between the button and comb, and the other end counterclockwise. Twist the ends together once or twice and trim them short enough to stay tucked under the button.

2. Repeat Step 1 to attach as many more like or different-size buttons as you wish.

3. To finish, top each of the larger flower buttons with a coconut button center. Simply apply a good dab of tacky glue to the back and then press the button in place. Let the glue dry thoroughly, and the comb is ready to wear.

Necklaces, Pins, Bracelets, and Rings

Sea Star Pendant

For as long as the villagers of Motunui could remember, the waters surrounding their island home were filled with fantastic sea creatures. Modeled after one of those reef residents, this faux pearl-studded clay starfish pendant makes a striking necklace.

Materials:

- One ¾-inch ball and one small pearl-size ball of tan or off-white polymer clay
- Disposable plastic knife
- Clay-decorating ball tool
- 1½-inch silver-plaited eye pin
- Aluminum foil
- Brown acrylic craft paint
- Craft paintbrush
- Glue sealer
- Tacky glue
- White faux pearl beads (one 5/16 inch and five ¼ inch)
- Beading cord thin enough to thread three pieces through the eye pin
- Decorative button (about 5/8 inch wide)

Instructions:

1. Press the clay into a flat disk about 1¼ inches wide and 1/8 inch thick. Use the knife to cut five equally spaced notches from the outer edge halfway to the center. Shape each of the five sections into an elongated, slightly curved sea star arm.

2. Insert the eye pin into the sea star, gently pushing it from the left side of the top arm through the inner clay diagonally down into the lower right arm. Gently push the clay surrounding the pin close to the metal to keep if from falling out of the sea star after you bake it.

3. Use the ball tool to make a 3/8-inch-wide depression in the center of the sea star. Then press a row of four smaller holes down the middle of each arm, extending from the center depression all the way to the tip.

4. Place the pearl-sized ball of clay into the center depression and use the ball tool to gently tamp it in place to create a thin decorative lip.

5. Bake the sea star in the oven or a toaster oven on a foil-lined tray according to the manufacturer's directions.

6. When the clay has completely cooled, brush the entire surface with a wash of diluted brown craft paint. Use the tip of the brush to fill the outer three holes in each arm with a bit of undiluted paint.

7. Let the paint dry. Then seal the sea star with a coat or two of glue sealer, and let it dry thoroughly.

8. Use tacky glue to stick the largest pearl bead in place in the center depression and the five smaller ones into the immediate surrounding holes.

9. Once the glue is set, cut three pieces of beading cord several inches longer than the desired length of your necklace. Thread them through the eye of the pendant pin and slide the sea star to the center.

10. Braid the cords together on one side of the pendant. When you are about an inch from the end, thread on the button "fastener" and knot the cords behind it.

11. Braid the cords on the other side of the pendant, this time knotting them together two inches from the ends. Tie a second knot a little ways below the first to create a loop just big enough for the button to slip through, and the pendant is ready to wear.

Ribbon Lei

A popular variation of the famous leis of the Pacific Islands, this braided ribbon necklace can be given and worn at all kinds of special occasions, such as weddings, birthdays, and graduations. Colorful and lasting, it is a wonderful demonstration of love, affection, and friendship.

Materials:
- 2 contrasting colors of ribbon
- (¼ to ½ inch wide)
- Sewing tape or ruler
- Scissors

Instructions:

1. Measure and cut a piece of ribbon in each color that is five times longer than the desired length of the lei.

2. Tie the two ribbons together with an overhand knot 4 or 5 inches from one end. You'll use the loose tails later to join the two ends of the finished lei.

3. Now it's time to weave the ribbons together. Hold the knot with the tails trailing down. Make a small loop with the left ribbon just above the knot. Wrap the right ribbon once around the base of the loop. Then make a loop with the same (right) ribbon and slip it through the first loop.

4. Gently pull on the left ribbon to tighten it. Then use it to make another loop to slip through the second loop. Pull on the right ribbon to tighten it.

5. Continue in this manner, slipping each new loop into the last and tightening the ribbons, until you have 4 or 5 inches of ribbon left.

6. Thread the ribbon that you would have used for the next loop all the way through the last loop, and tighten the loop.

7. Tie the four ribbon tails together to complete the lei.

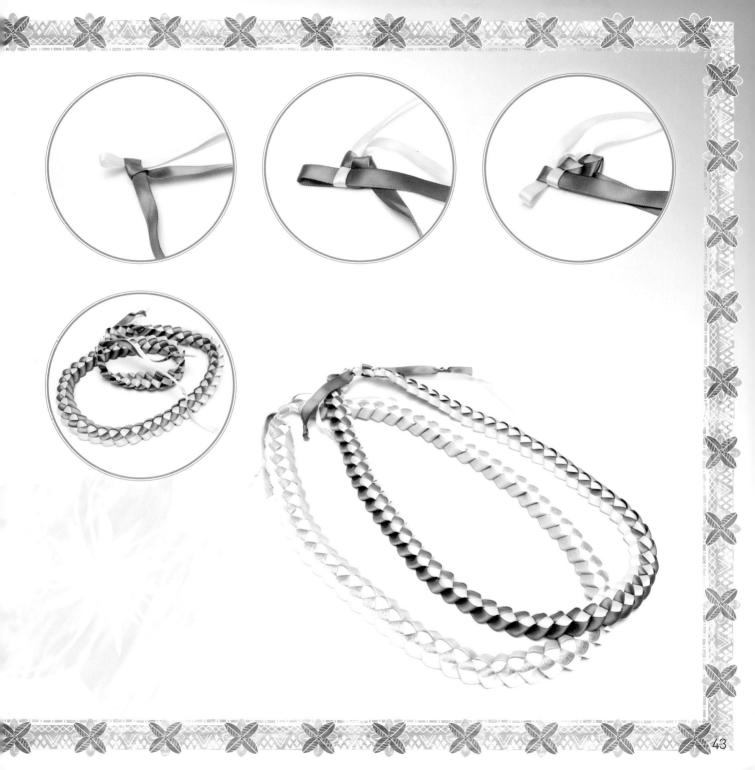

Paper Tattoo Rings

Maui the demigod is covered with tattoos—including a Mini Maui tattoo who comes alive to explain all of Maui's illustrated feats. These rings are inspired by Maui's lively tattoos and are decorated with a zigzag motif to represent sharks' teeth.

Materials:
- Craft paper (tan, black, and other solid colors)
- Ruler
- Decorative-edged (zigzag) craft scissors or pinking shears
- Regular straight-edged scissors
- Fine-tipped permanent marker
- Glue stick
- Glue sealer and small paintbrush to apply it

Instructions:

1. For each ring, cut a 1- by 3-inch strip of tan paper (or another shade you like). Tip: You can make the ring a little wider if you like, but not too much or it will be hard to shape into a circle.

2. Fold over both of the long edges ¼ inch to create a ½-inch strip.

3. Use the craft scissors to cut one or two thin 3-inch-long zigzag strips from black or colored paper. Then use the glue stick to attach the zigzag strip to the front of the ring strip. If you like, use the marker to draw on a thin decorative line above the zigzag.

4. Brush a coat of glue sealer on the front and back of the assembled ring strip and let it dry completely.

5. Shape the decorated strip into a ring, and fit one end under the folded flaps of the opposite end. Slide the inserted end further in or out to adjust the size to fit.

Woven Fish Pin

The lagoons surrounding Motunui are filled with fish of all colors, shapes, and sizes. Here's a fun weaving technique for netting a colorful fish to pin on a sweater, jacket, backpack, or purse.

Materials:
- Paper-covered craft wire
- Craft pliers/wire cutters
- Thin colored cord or twine (20-pound works well)
- Measuring tape
- Scissors
- Toothpick
- Small rectangular scrap of felt
- Low-temperature glue gun
- ¾-inch bar pin

Instructions:

1. Cut a 5½-inch length of the wire to make a 2½-inch long fish. For a smaller fish, decrease the length a half inch or so.

2. Bend the wire in the center and cross the ends over each other to create a simple fish shape.

3. Cut a 36-inch length of cord or twine. Tie one end around the crossed wires to secure them. Then, weave the long end across the body of the fish, wrapping it alternately around the top wire and then the bottom so that the middle fills in with crisscrossed cords. Stop ¼ to ½ inch from the front of the head.

4. Knot the cord end around one of the wires and trim it an inch or so from the knot. Use the tip of the toothpick to tuck the loose cord ends at both ends of the fish into the weave.

5. Hot glue a small rectangle of felt to the back of the woven section of the fish. Then, carefully apply a line of hot glue to the top of the bar pin and stick it to the felt.

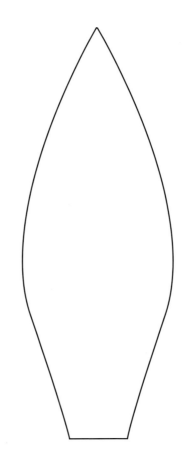

Leafy Bun Wrap
Template